THE
Chocolate
SOLDIER

THE

Chocolate

SOLDIER

Heroism: The Lost Chord of Christianity

C.T. STUDD

Deeper Christian Press
Christ-Centered Teaching and Resources

The Chocolate Soldier – *Heroism: The Lost Chord of Christianity*
by C.T. Studd

978-1-953549-02-0 (print)
978-1-953549-03-7 (ebook)

Deeper Christian Press
PO Box 654 | Windsor, CO 80550

Published in the United States of America.

deeperChristian.com
This ministry is maintained by the Lord
through the stewardship of those who value it.

CONTENTS

Foreword by NRJohnson   7

The Chocolate Soldier   9

Only One Life, Twill Soon Be Past   33

Quaint Rhymes for the Battlefield
    The Bible   39
    Jesus Only   45
    Chutney   51
    Christian's Delight   55
    Without Excuse   63
    God's DD   67

C.T. Studd Quotes   71

FOREWORD

I was first introduced to this mighty hero of old by my friend Eric Ludy. Soon thereafter, Norman Grubb's well written biography of C.T. Studd helped me gain an understanding of Studd's passion and perseverance through every difficulty imaginable. And yet Studd's continual boast was:

> Difficulties, dangers, disease, death, or divisions don't deter any but Chocolate [soldiers] from executing God's Will. When someone says there's a lion in the way, the real Christian promptly replies, "That's hardly enough inducement for me; I want a bear or two besides to make it worth my while to go."

Reading the words of C.T. Studd (1860-1931)—Britain's famous cricketer and missionary to China, India, and Africa—is no easy endeavor. The words are simple but each phrase is packed with a punch that leaves you reeling, convicted, and yet oddly inspired. If Studd argued that his day was filled with "namby-pamby lukewarm" Chocolate Christians, I fear what he would say about our generation today. And yet his call couldn't be more needed: be a true soldier of Jesus Christ and plunge headlong into the world in the power of His Spirit, to proclaim the Gospel and live out the true, historic, and victorious Christian life. This deeperChristian classic edition includes:

- *The Chocolate Soldier* — or also known as: *Heroism: The Lost Chord of Christianity*
- *Only One Life, Twill Soon Be Past* (a famous poem by Studd)
- A collection of poems Studd wrote entitled *Quaint Rhymes for the Battlefield*
- A collection of our favorite C.T. Studd quotes

Studd's life continues to challenge and confront my comfortable Christianity and lackadaisical living. May his words do the same for you.

NRJohnson
deeperChristian.com

THE CHOCOLATE SOLDIER

Heroism is the lost chord; the missing note of present-day Christianity!

Every true soldier is a hero! **A soldier without heroism is a chocolate soldier!** Who has not been stirred to scorn and mirth at the very thought of a Chocolate Soldier? In peace true soldiers are captive lions, fretting in their cages. War gives them their liberty and sends them, like boys bounding out of school, to obtain their heart's desire or perish in the attempt. Battle is the soldier's vital breath! Peace turns him into a stooping asthmatic. War makes him a whole man again, and gives him the heart, strength, and vigour of a hero.

Every true Christian is a soldier — of Christ — a hero "par excellence!" Braver than the bravest — scorning the soft seductions of peace and her oft-repeated warnings against hardship, disease, danger, and death, whom he counts among his bosom friends.

The otherwise Christian is a Chocolate Christian! Dissolving in water and melting at the smell of fire. "Sweeties" they are! Bonbons, lollipops! Living their lives on a glass dish or in a cardboard box, each clad in his soft clothing, a little frilled white paper to preserve his dear little delicate constitution.

Here are some portraits of Chocolate Soldiers taken by the Lord Jesus Christ Himself.

"He said, 'I go sir,' and went not." He said he would go to the heathen, but he stuck fast to Christendom instead.

"They say and do not" — they tell others to go, and yet do not go themselves. "Never," said General Gordon to a corporal, as he himself jumped upon the parapet of a trench before Sebastopol to fix a gabion which the corporal had ordered a private to fix and would not fix himself, "Never tell another man to do what you are afraid to do yourself."

To the Chocolate Christian the very thought of war brings a violent attack of ague, while the call to battle always finds him with the palsy. "I really cannot move," he says. "I only wish I could, but I can sing, and here are some of my favorite lines:

> I must be carried to the skies
> On a flowery bed of ease,
> Let others fight to win the prize,
> Or sail thro' bloody seas.

> Mark time, Christian heroes,
> Never go to war;
> Stop and mind the babies
> Playing on the floor.

> Wash and dress and feed them
> Forty times a week.
> Till they're roly poly —
> Puddings so to speak.

Chorus:
Round and round the nursery
Let us ambulate,
Sugar and spice and all that's nice
Must be on our slate."

"Thank the good Lord," said a very fragile, white-haired lady, "God never meant me to be a jellyfish!" She wasn't!

• • • • •

God never was a chocolate manufacturer, and never will be. God's men are always heroes. In Scripture you can trace their giant foot-tracks down the sands of time.

NOAH

Noah walked with God, he did not only preach righteousness, he acted it. He went through water and did not melt. He breasted the current of the popular opinion of his day, scorning alike the hatred and ridicule of the scoffers who mocked at the thought of there being but one way of salvation. He warned the unbelieving and, entering the ark himself, did not open the door an inch when once God had shut it. A real hero untainted by the fear of man!

Learn to scorn the praise of men.
Learn to lose with God;
Jesus won the world through shame!
And beckons us His road.

11

ABRAHAM

Abraham, a simple farmer, at a word from the Invisible God, marched, with family and stock, through the terrible desert to a distant land to live among a people whose language he could neither speak nor understand! Not bad that! But later he did even better, marching hot foot against the combined armies of five kings, flushed with recent victory, to rescue one man! His army? Just 318 odd fellows, armed like a circus crowd. And he won too! "He always wins who sides with God." What pluck! Only a farmer! No war training! Yet what hero has eclipsed his fear? His open secret? He was the friend of God.

MOSES

Moses the man of God — was a species of human chameleon — scholar, general, law-giver, leader, etc. Brought up as the Emperor's grandson with more than a good chance of coming to the throne, one thing only between him and it — Truth — what a choice! What a temptation! A throne for a lie! Ignominy, banishment, or likely enough death for the truth! He played the man! "Refusing to be called the son of Pharaoh's daughter, he chose rather to suffer affliction with the people of God than to enjoy the pleasures of sin and success for a season, accounting the reproach of Christ greater riches than the treasures of Egypt."

Again I see him. Now an old man and alone, marching stolidly back to Egypt after forty years of exile, to beard the lion in his den, to liberate Pharaoh's slaves right under his very nose, and to lead them across that great and terrible wilderness. A wild-cat affair, if ever there was one! When were God's schemes otherwise? Look at Jordan, Jericho,

Gideon, Goliath, and scores of others. Tame tabby-cat schemes are stamped with another hallmark — that of the Chocolate Brigade! How dearly they love their tabbies, yet think themselves wise men! **Real Christians revel in desperate ventures for Christ, expecting from God great things and attempting the same with exhilaration.** History cannot match this feat of Moses. How was it done? He consulted not with flesh and blood; he obeyed not men but God.

Once again I see the old grey-beard, this time descending Mount Sinai with giant strides and rushing into the camp, his eyes blazing like burning coals. One man against two million dancing dervishes drunk with debauchery! Bravo! Well done, old man! First class! His cheek does not pale, but his mouth moves, and I think I catch his words, "If God is for me, who can be against me? I will not be afraid of 10,000 of the people that have set themselves against me. Though a host should encamp against me, my heart shall not fear." And he didn't. He wins again. Whence this desperate courage? Listen! "Now the man Moses was very meek above all the men which were upon the face of the earth." "The Lord spoke to Moses face to face, as a man speaks to his friend." "My servant Moses," said his Master, "is faithful in all Mine house; with him I will speak mouth to mouth." Such is the explanation of Moses, the chameleon, the man and friend of God, and consequently a first-class hero.

DAVID

David, the man after God's own heart, was a man of war and a mighty man of valour. When all Israel were on the run, David faced Goliath — alone ... with God — and he but a stripling, and well scolded too by his brother for having come to see the battle. What a splendid fool Eliab must have been! as though David would go to see a battle and not stay to fight. **They are chocolate soldiers who merely go to see battles, and coolly urge others to fight them.** They had better save their journey money and use it to send out real fighters instead. Soldiers don't need dry nurses, and if they did the Holy Spirit is always on the spot and ready to undertake any case on simple application. No! David went to the battle and stayed to fight, and won! Wise beyond his years, he had no use for Saul's armour. It cramped his freedom of action. He tried it on and took it off, quick sharp. And, besides, it made such a ghastly rattle, even when he walked, that he could not hear the still small voice of God, and would never have heard Him saying afterwards, "This is the way to the brook, David! and there are the five smooth stones! Trust only in Me and them. Your own home-made sling will do first class, and there! that's the shortest cut to Goliath." The chocolates ran away — they were all Chocolates — but David ran upon Goliath. One smooth stone was enough.

David's secret was that he had but one Director, and He, the Infallible One. He directed the stone, as He directed the youth. Too many directors spoil the sport, and two are too many by just one. Thus Christ said to His soldiers: "HE shall teach you all things, HE shall guide you into all the truth."

"THIS is My Beloved Son: HEAR HIM."

"ONE MEDIATOR ONLY, between God and Man, the man Christ Jesus."

One director of Christian men — God the Holy Spirit. Whose directions require indeed instant obedience, but not the endorsement of any man.

The devil needs a red-hot shot, fresh from the foundry of the Holy Spirit. He laughs at cold shot or tepid, and as for that made of half-iron and half-clay, half-divine and half-human, why you might just as well pelt him with snowballs.

Whence did this raw youth derive his pluck and skill? Not from military camps, nor theological schools, nor religious retreats. "To know The Only True God and Jesus Christ," is enough. Paul determined to know only Jesus Christ, and look at the grand result! Whilst others were learning pretty theories, David, like John [the Baptist], had been alone with God in the wilds, practicing on bears and lions. **The result? He knew God and did exploits. He knew God only. He trusted God only. He obeyed God only. That's the secret. God alone gives strength.** God adulterated with men entails the weakness of iron and clay — Chocolate — brittleness!

Yet hero as he was, even David alas! once played the role of Chocolate Soldier. He stayed at home when he should have gone to war. His army, far off, in danger, fighting the enemy, won. David, at home, secure, within sight of God's house and often going there, suffered the one great defeat of his life, entailing such a bitter, life-long reaping as might well deter others from the folly of sowing wild oats. David's sin is a terrific sermon (like Lot's preaching in Sodom must have been), its theme — **"Don't be a Chocolate Soldier!"**

In his simple, quick, and full confession, David proved himself a man again. It takes a real man to make a true confession — a Chocolate Soldier will excuse or cloak his sin. He tumbles in the mud, flounders on, wipes his mouth to try to get the bad taste of his acted lie out of it, and then goes on his way saying, "I have done no wickedness." A self-murdering fool! Killing his conscience to save his face, like Balaam beating the donkey who sought to save his master's life. Being a Chocolate Soldier nearly did for David. Beware!

NATHAN

Nathan was another real Christian Soldier. He went to his king and rebuked him to his face, like Peter's dealing with Ananias (only David embraced his opportunity and confessed), and unlike the Chocolate Soldiers of today who go whispering about and refusing either to judge, rebuke, or put away evil because of the entailed scandal forsooth. Veritable Soapy Sams. They say "It is nothing! nothing at all! A mere misunderstanding!" As though God's cause would suffer more through a bold declaration and defense of the truth and the use of the knife, than by the hiding up of sin, and the certain development of mortification in the member, involving death to the whole body. "He that doeth righteousness is righteous," and "he that doeth sin is of the devil," and ought to be told so. He that is a second time led captive by the devil needs neither plaster nor treacle, but the brace rebuke and summons to repentance of a righteous man to effect his salvation. We are badly in need of Nathans today, who fear God and nought else, no, not even a scandal.

DANIEL

Daniel was another hero. Of course he was! Was he not the man greatly beloved of God who sent an angel to tell him so?

I love to watch him as he walks, with firm step and

radiant face, to the lions' den, stopping but once — like his Master *en route* to Calvary — to comfort his weeping and agonized emperor. God shut the mouths of the lions against Daniel, but opened them wide against those who had opened their mouths against His servant.

A man is known by his works, and the works of Daniel were his three friends, who, rather than bow down to men or gold, braved the fiery furnace.

Again we see him going to the banquet hall, and hear his conductor whisper in his ear, "Draw it mild, Daniel, be statesmanlike. Place and power again for you if you are tactful and wise — especially tactful!" And Daniel's simple reply, "Get thee behind me, Satan!" There he stands before the king, braving torture or instant death — but it's the king who quails, not Daniel — who tells him to his face the whole hot truth of God, diminishing not a jot.

JOHN THE BAPTIST

John the Baptist, a man taught and made and sent of God — good old John! Who doesn't love and admire him? Why, even Herod did. A genuine deficiency of oil and treacle in his composition. He always told the bang flat truth, with emphasis. As he loved, so he warned. He knew not how to fawn. He wooed with the sword, and "men" loved him the better for it. They always do.

The leaders of religion sent to John to ask him the dearly loved question of every Pharisee, "By what authority doest thou these (good) things?" They asked that of Christ Himself, and crucified Him for the doing of them. John's answer was plain and pungent, "I will tell you what you ask, and more. (John was always liberal!) I? I am nobody, but ye and your masters are a generation of vipers." A good hot curry, that! John never served his curries with butter sauce, but he was always very liberal with chutney — a man of God — no sugar plum nor Chocolate Soldier he!

Thus also he faced Herod after six months in an underground dungeon, and he a man of "God's Open-air Mission." Brought straight in before the king; surrounded with all the might and majesty of camp and court; blinking at the unaccustomed sight of light, but by no means putting blinkers on the truth, he blurted out his hot and thunderous rebuke, "Thou shalt not have that woman to be thy wife." A whole sermon in one sentence, as easy to remember as impossible to forget. John had preached like that before; like Hugh Latimer, he was not above repeating a good sermon to a king, word for word, when the king had not given sufficient heed to it.

John received the unique distinction of a first-class character from both God and the agent of the devil. Hark to the Savior indulging in an outburst of exquisite sarcasm, "What think ye of John? A reed shaken by the wind? A man clothed in soft raiment?" A Chocolate Christian? (How delicious! The Chocolates were right in front of Jesus at the time — Pharisees, Sadducees, priests, scribes, lawyers, and other hypocrites. How the crowd must have enjoyed it!) "A prophet? Nay, much more than a prophet! Of men born of women there is none greater than John." And what did the devil's agent say when, after John's death, he heard of Jesus? "This, is John risen from the dead." What a character! Fancy Jesus being mistaken for anyone! He could have been mistaken only for John. Nobody envies him the well-deserved honour, great though it was, for John was a man — pure granite right through, with not a grain of chocolate in him.

Had John but heard Jesus say, "Ye shall be My witnesses unto the uttermost parts of the earth," I very much doubt if Herod's dungeon, or his soldiers, could have detained him. He surely would have found some means of escape, and run off to preach Christ's Gospel, if not in the very heart of Africa, then in some more difficult and dangerous place. Yet Christ said, referring to His subsequent gift of the Holy Spirit to every believer, "He that is least in the kingdom of God is greater than he," intimating that even greater powers than those of John are at the disposal of every Christian, and that what John was, each one of us can be — good, straight, bold, unconquerable, heroic.

PAUL
But here are other foot-tracks — outrageous ones: they can belong only to one man — that grandest of Christian paradoxes — the little giant Paul — whose head was as big as his body, and his heart greater than both. Once he thought and treated every Christian as a combination of knave and fool. Then he became one himself. He was called "fool" because his acts were so far beyond the dictates of human reason, and "mad" because of his irresponsible fiery zeal for Christ and men. A first-class scholar, but one who knew how to use scholarship properly; for he put it on the shelf, declaring the wisdom of men to be but folly, and determined to know nothing else save Jesus Christ and Him crucified. **The result — he made the world turn somersault.** His life was a perpetual gamble for God. Daily he faced death for Christ. Again and again he stood fearless before crowds thirsting for his blood. He stood before kings and governors and "turned not a hair." He didn't so much as flinch before

Nero, that vice-president of hell. His sufferings were appalling; read them. He trod in his Master's footsteps, and so received — God is always just in His favors — the same splendid compliment that Jesus did. "All forsook him." So there were some Chocolate Christians in those days too. Anyone who forsook Paul must have been made of Chocolate. Doubtless the "CHOCOLATES" excused themselves as they do today. "Who could abide such a fanatical, fiery fool? such an uncompromising character? Nobody could work with him, or he with them!" (What a lie! Jesus did, and they got on well together.) A tactless enthusiast, who considered it his business to tell every man the unvarnished truth regardless of consequences. He won his degree hands down, and without a touch of the spur. A first-class one, too — that of the headman's axe — next best to that of the cross.

· · · · ·

And so the tale goes on. Go where you will through the Scriptures or history, you find that men who really knew God, and didn't merely say they did, were invariably Paragons of Pluck; Dare-Devil Desperadoes for Jesus; Gamblers for God. "Fools and Madmen," shout the world and the Chocolates. "Yes, for Christ's sake," add the Angels!

Nobly they fought to win the prize,
Climbing the steep ascents of heaven,
Thro' peril, toil, and pain.
O God, to us let grace be given,
To follow in their train.

• • • • •

The Chocolate Christians of today can at least boast of having ancient pedigrees.

CHOCOLATES A LA REUBEN

There are Chocolates a la Reuben (Judges 5:16), who have great searchings of heart, and make great resolves of heart too. But somehow they still sit among the sheepfolds, listening to the pipings of their much-loved organs and church choirs. It's good to have a great heartsearching. It's better to make a great heart-resolve. But, if instead of obeying, we squat among the sheep, leaving our few hard-pressed brethren to tackle the wolves by themselves, verily we are but Chocolate Christians. You made a great resolve to go to Africa for Christ a year or two ago. Where are you now? In England? Yes! Yes! Lollipop!

CHOCOLATES MEROZ

There are Chocolates Meroz (Judges 5:23), who earned the curse of the angel of the Lord. War was declared; the battle about to begin; the odds were outrageous, and Meroz remained in England attending conventions until the battle was over, then he went, in comfort and security, as a Cook's tourist! Doubtless they said, "They couldn't fight till they had been properly ordained, and, besides, there was so very much to be done in fat, overfed Meroz, and surely to feed a flock of fat sheep in a safe place has always been considered the ideal training of war"; as though the best training for the soldier was to become a nurse-maid!!!

CHOCOLATES DU BALAAM

Chocolates Du Balaam (Numbers 22-24) begin first-class, and earn the name of prophets. Then they develop a squint, melt, and finally run out of the frying-pan into the fire, thus Balaam.

One day he couldn't get his left eye to look at God. It would look at earth and mammon and that chit of a girl, Miss Popularity. He ought to have done as God told him, and plucked it out. But he said that was too much to ask of any man, and besides he wanted the best of both worlds. He had a hearty desire to die the death of the righteous, but he wasn't willing to pay the price of a righteous life. He hadn't the pluck to curse God's people, so he made plans for others to make them sin. But one day, while his dupes were putting his chestnuts into the fire, they fell in themselves, and Balaam with them.

"I counsel thee to buy of me eyesalve, that thou mayest once again have a single eye, and be enabled to see the folly of flirting with the world."

CHOCOLATE DEMAS

Chocolate Demas (2 Timothy 4:10), who left old fiery hard-hitting Paul for an easier path. He said he thought Paul should wink at, or slobber over sin, instead of rebuking it. "He was so very fond of the knife, you know; and he never would use sticking-plaster, because he said it never healed the sore but made it burrow underneath and become bigger, worse, and dangerous."

MARK

Mark (Acts 13:13) joined the Chocolate Brigade once.

He left Paul and Barnabas in the lurch, and went back to Jerusalem for a rest cure — a religious retreat. Thank God he got sick of it ere long, resigned his commission, and re-enlisting in God's army became a useful soldier.

OLD PROPHETS

Many fine youngsters are turned into chocolates by old prophets (1 Kings 13). Old prophets who have lost their fire, or fire off words instead of deeds, usually become Great Chocolate Manufacturers. That poor young prophet. He did so well when he obeyed God only, but it was all over with him when he listened to another voice, even though that of an old prophet. Didn't the old prophet say he was a prophet? and say he'd got the message straight from God? What a damnable lie! The floor of Christendom and elsewhere is littered with wrecks made by old prophets. God won't stand nonsense from any man. Every man has to choose between Christ and Barabbas, and every Christian between God and some old prophet. Better be a silly donkey in the estimation of an old prophet than listen to his soft talk and flattery, and afterwards become a wreck. "This is My beloved Son, hear HIM." No! not even Moses, nor Elijah, nor both. "HEAR HIM." "You have an anointing from God, and you have no need that any man teach you." You say you believe the Bible! do your deeds give the lie to your words?

THE TEN SPIES

The ten spies were chocolates (Numbers 13). They melted and ran over the whole congregation of Israel, turning them into Chocolate Creams — "softies," afraid to face the fire and water before them. God put them all into the saucepan again and boiled them for forty years in the desert, and left them there. He has no use for Chocolates. It's not small things He despises, but "Chocolates"; for He said, "Your little ones shall inherit the promised land which you have forfeited through listening to men and despising Me."

JONAH

Jonah (Jonah 1) became a Chocolate Soldier once. Told to go to Africa, he went to Liverpool and took ship for America. Luckily he met a storm and a whale which, after three days' instruction, taught him how to pray and obey, and set him once again on the right track.

• • • • •

There's nothing that shows up Chocolates so much as a bit of a breeze [argument] among God's people. Paul and Barnabas had one once. Judging from experience, I guess there were some Chocolates about then who got into a fog right away! Before that, they had vowed they would go to the heathen; but this breeze between P. and B. put them off. If they hadn't been made of chocolate they would have said, "This affair between Paul and Barnabas only makes it more necessary for me to keep close to God, and do what He told me to do more exactly and punctually; so I shall go a bit sooner to Africa — that's all!"

Difficulties, dangers, disease, death, or divisions don't deter any but Chocolates from executing God's Will. When someone says there's a lion in the

way, the real Christian promptly replies, "That's hardly enough inducement for me; I want a bear or two besides to make it worth my while to go."

Chocolates are very fond of talking loud and long against some whom they call fanatics, as though there were any danger of Christians being fanatics nowadays! Why, fanatics among Christians are as rare as the "dodo." Now, if they declaimed against "tepidity," they would talk sense. God's real people have always been called fanatics. Jesus was called mad; so was Paul; so was Whitfield, Wesley, Moody, and Spurgeon. No one has graduated far in God's School who has not been paid the compliment of being called a fanatic. We Christians of today are indeed a tepid crew. Had we but half the fire and enthusiasm of the Suffragettes in the past, we would have the world evangelized and Christ back among us in no time.

Had we the pluck and heroism of the Flyers, or the men who volunteered for the North or South Polar Expeditions, or for the Great War, or for any ordinary dare-devil enterprise, we could have every soul on earth knowing the name and salvation of Jesus Christ in less than ten years.

Alas! What stirs ordinary men's blood and turns them into heroes, makes most Christians run like a flock of frightened sheep. The Militants daily risked their lives in furtherance of their cause, and subscribed of their means in a way that cried "Shame" on us Christians, who generally brand the braving of risks and fighting against odds as a "tempting of God."

Chocolate Carmels — "stick-jaw," boys call

them — jawing, "I go, sir," and sticking fast in Christendom. No conquest is made in assured safety, and conquest for Christ certainly cannot so be made.

· · · · ·

We Christians too often **substitute prayer for playing the game.** Prayer is good: but when used as a substitute for obedience, it is naught but a blatant hypocrisy, a despicable Pharisaism. We need as many meetings for action as for prayer — perhaps more. Every orthodox prayer-meeting is opened by God saying to His people, "Go work today; pray that labourers be sent into My vineyard." It is continued by the Christian's response, "I go, Lord, whithersoever Thou sendest me, that Thy Name may be hallowed everywhere, that Thy Kingdom may come speedily, that Thy Will may be done on earth as in heaven." But if it ends in nobody going anywhere, it had better never have been held at all. Like faith, prayer without works is dead. That is why many prayer-meetings might well be styled "much cry, yet little wool." Zerubbabel didn't only hold prayer-meetings; he went and cut down trees, and started to build. Hence God said, "From this day will I bless thee."

Report says that someone has rediscovered the secret of the old masters. Cannot we Christians rediscover, and put into practice, that of our Great Master and His former pupils, Heroism? He and they saved not themselves; they loved not their lives to the death, and so kept on saving them by losing them for Christ's sake.

We are frittering away time and money in a multiplicity of conventions, conferences, and retreats, when the real need is to go straight and full steam into battle, with the signal for "close action" flying.

The "Vox Humana" plays too important a part in our Christian organs and organizations today. The music, whoever plays, is bound to be thin when the tops of "Instant Obedience" and "Fiery Valor" are missing or unused, and without them to play the "Lost Chord" of Heroism is an impossibility.

"Whatsoever he saith unto you, do it," said the Blessed Virgin. Do what? Not put treacle and spice into the soft holy vessels inside the house, but pour the Water of Life into those empty stone ones outside. Cana's marriage feast would have ended in shame had the wine run short. Christ's marriage feast begins only when the wine is sufficient — a blend from every tongue and kindred and tribe and nation. The supply is assured, as soon as the water is poured out as Christ directed, into "the uttermost parts of the earth." The mischief today is the reluctance of the servants to do the outside work. They all want to serve indoors, wear smart clothes, listen to the conversation, and make a terrible lot of themselves in the butler's pantry.

LET US MAKE A REAL START NOW — AT ONCE

For years, like Mr. Winkle, we've declared we were just about to begin, and then never began at all.

We must divorce Chocolate and Disobedience, and marry Faith and Heroism.

"Who shall begin the battle?" asked the king. "Thou," replied the prophet, and when the king and the young princes led the way, though the odds against them were terrific, they won with ridiculous ease. So, too, the Apostles led in the war of God to the uttermost parts of the earth. Likewise in the Crusades, the kings and princes of State and Church led; then why not today in the crusade of Christ to evangelize the world?

God's summons today is to the young men and women of Great Britain and America and Christendom, who call themselves by the name of Christ. "New wine," said Christ, "must be placed in New bottles." Those superfluously labelled and patched-up old-fashioned ones are as hopeless as the New Theology. They can't be moved lest they burst with pride and spill the wine in the wrong place.

Listen: "And it shall be in the last days, I will pour forth of My Spirit upon all flesh. Your sons and your daughters shall prophesy, your young men shall see visions (of faith), your old men shall dream dreams (of valorous obedience); yea, and on My bondmen and on my bondmaidens in those days will I pour forth of My Spirit, and they shall prophesy; and I will show wonders in the heaven above and signs in the earth beneath;...and it shall be that whosoever shall call on the name of the Lord shall be saved" (Acts 2:17-21). But how can they call on Him of whom they have not even heard? Must you stay, young man? Can't you go, young woman, and tell them? Verily we are in the last — the Laodicean stage — that of the Lukewarm Church.

Wilt thou be to Christ the partner of His throne or an emetic (Revelation 3:21); a Militant or a Chocolate Christian? Wilt thou fear or wilt thou fight? Shall your brethren go to war and shall ye sit here? When He comes, shall He find faith on the earth?

A thousand times you have admitted Christ's
Love so amazing, so divine,
Demands your life, your soul, your all.
Wilt thou be a miser and withhold what honour

demands of thee? Wilt thou give like Ananias and Sapphira, who, pretending to give all, gave only part?

Possessing and enjoying the vineyard, wilt thou, like the husbandman, refuse the agreed rent? Wilt thou fear death, or devil, or men? AND WILT THOU NOT FEAR SHAME?

Some shall rise to everlasting life, and some to shame and everlasting contempt.

Shall we refuse to emulate the heroes of old, or shall we accomplish the double fulfillment of those glorious words? —

All these being men of war came with a perfect heart to make Jesus King over all the world. They were all mighty men of valor for the war! He that was least was equal to a hundred, and the greatest to a thousand! They were not of double heart! Their faces were like the faces of lions! They were as swift as the roes upon the mountains (to do their Lord's commands)! Ye sought in time past, for Jesus to be King over you. **Now, then, do it** (Compare 1 Chronicles 12:8, 33, 38, and 2 Samuel 3:17-18).

Shall we not reply: We are Yours, Jesus, and on Your side. God do so to me, and more also, if as God has sworn unto Him, I do not even so to Jesus — to translate the kingdom from the house of Satan, and set up the throne of Jesus Christ over all the world (Compare 1 Chronicles 12:18 and 2 Samuel 3:10).

Come, then, let us restore the "Lost Chord" of Christianity — **HEROISM** — to the world, and the crown of the world to Christ. Christ Himself asks thee, "Wilt thou be a Malingerer or a Militant?"

• • • • •

To your knees, man! and to your Bible! Decide at once! Don't hedge! Time flies! Cease your insults to God, quit consulting flesh and blood. Stop your lame, lying, and cowardly excuses.

Enlist! Here are your papers and oath of allegiance. Scratch out one and sign the other in the presence of God and the recording angel. Mark God's endorsements underneath.

HENCEFORTH

For me	**For Me**
To live is Christ.	Chocolate my name.
To die is gain.	Tepidity my temperature.
I'll be a militant.	A malingerer I.
A man of God.	A child of men.
A gambler for Christ.	A self-excuser.
A hero.	A humbug.
SIGN HERE	SIGN HERE
_____	_____

God's promises are sure in either case: "Lo, I am with you always" or "I will spew thee out of My mouth."

Good Lord!
Baptize us with the Holy Spirit and with fire:
Cure us of this dread plague of Sleeping Sickness,
this crazy talking in our sleep, that even as we
unceasingly pray,

Thy Name be hallowed everywhere;
Thy Kingdom come speedily;
Thy Will will be done on earth, as it is in heaven.
Amen and Amen!

ONLY ONE LIFE, TWILL SOON BE PAST

Two little lines I heard one day,
Traveling along life's busy way;
Bringing conviction to my heart,
And from my mind would not depart;
Only one life, 'twill soon be past,
Only what's done for Christ will last.

Only one life, yes only one,
Soon will its fleeting hours be done;
Then, in "that day" my Lord to meet,
And stand before His Judgement seat;
Only one life, 'twill soon be past,
Only what's done for Christ will last.

Only one life, the still small voice,
Gently pleads for a better choice
Bidding me selfish aims to leave,
And to God's holy will to cleave;
Only one life, 'twill soon be past,
Only what's done for Christ will last.

Only one life, a few brief years,
Each with its burdens, hopes, and fears;
Each with its clays I must fulfill.
living for self or in His will;
Only one life, 'twill soon be past,
Only what's done for Christ will last.

When this bright world would tempt me sore,
When Satan would a victory score;
When self would seek to have its way,
Then help me Lord with joy to say;
Only one life, 'twill soon be past,
Only what's done for Christ will last.

Give me Father, a purpose deep,
In joy or sorrow Thy word to keep;
Faithful and true what e'er the strife,
Pleasing Thee in my daily life;
Only one life, 'twill soon be past,
Only what's done for Christ will last.

Oh let my love with fervor burn,
And from the world now let me turn;
Living for Thee, and Thee alone,
Bringing Thee pleasure on Thy throne;
Only one life, 'twill soon be past,
Only what's done for Christ will last.

Only one life, yes only one,
Now let me say, "Thy will be done";
And when at last I'll hear the call,
I know I'll say "twas worth it all";

Only one life, twill soon be past,
Only what's done for Christ will last.

• • • • •

Only one life, 'twill soon be past,
Only what's done for Christ will last.
And when I am dying, how happy I'll be,
If the lamp of my life has been burned out for Thee.

QUAINT RHYMES FOR THE BATTLEFIELD

THE BIBLE

What could we do without the Book
That God gave us to read?
No more than any farmer
Who hadn't any seed!

No other tells us of our Lord,
The God of grace and love,
Who made the whole creation,
This world and those above.

What could we do were we without
The Gospels or the Acts?
No more than could a barrister
Who didn't know his facts!

Were we without the letters of
John, Peter, James and Paul,
We'd be like some poor cricketer
Without a bat or ball.

If Genesis is humbug,
We must cast into the flames
The Gospels, Acts and Hebrews,
Galatians, Romans, James.

If we should try to live our lives
Without the Book of Psalms,
Our souls would lack the music
Which comforts, cheers and charms.

We couldn't know that God will be
The Judge of all mankind,
By the mere dictates of Reason,
Or the workings of the mind.

We shouldn't know God gave His Son,
To agonise and die,
To save and teach us sinful men
To trust Him utterly.

We shouldn't know Christ rose again —
The proof He was the Lord —
And then ascended up above
To execute His Word.

We ne'er had deemed He'd be the Friend
Of publicans and sinners,
Of prodigals and harlots, not
Of hypocrites nor trimmers.

That ne'er would He to any child
Deny a Saviour's blessing,
And ne'er would turn a soul away,
Who came his sins confessing.

That He Who healed the sick, the lame,
The blind, the deaf, the dumb,

And raised the dead, by touch or word,
Would beg us all to come

To Him, that we might be forgiven
And made the heirs of God,
Divorced from fear of death and hell,
Warriors of the Lord.

We ne'er had dreamed Salvation is
A gift, and not a wage,
To be received just as you are,
Without the sacred page.

The Bible is a gallery
Of pictures full of life,
A cinematographic show
Of real historic strife.

It warns against temptations
And Satan's savoury messes;
It paints the devil's portrait
In all his fancy dresses.

It's like a cordite rifle
With a telescopic sight,
Preventing those of single eye
From missing, day or night.

It is of heaven's narrow way
The ordnance survey map,
Revealing hell's paved broadway
And every gin and trap.

It gives the words of prophets,
Who courageously denounced
The sins of priests, and princes, and
The Judgment day announced.

It castigates the evil, and
It never screens the good;
It declares that every mortal needs
The Saviour's cleansing blood.

'Tis a history of the godly,
A hymn book for the saint,
A comfort to the dying,
A cordial to the faint.

It prophesies the Coming
Of the Saviour in His might,
To judge the world's inhabitants,
And darkness turn to light.

Be sure, in their originals,
Each word came straight from God;
"Yea! every jot and tittle's true,"
Said Jesus Christ the Lord.

Would you be brave and noble?
Read it every day,
Not as a duty merely,
Nor in a slipshod way.

Divorce yourself from humbug,
And cant and lollipops;

Don't live on milk and water,
Nor sentimental slops.

Don't be like Jackie Horner,
Who when he got a pie,
Picked out a plum or two, and said
"See what a boy am I!"

It's God's own patent medicine,
Take it as it stands;
Treat it as His aide-de-camp,
Bringing Christ's commands.

Mind! you must obey it,
Otherwise you'll be
Branded, as a hypocrite,
Through eternity.

Read it in the morning,
Meditate and pray,
Trust the Lord to keep you
"Straight" throughout the day.

JESUS ONLY

I'm going to live for Jesus,
And fling the world away,
I'm going to give to Jesus
   My life and all to-day.

I've done it, Hallelujah!
And now I pray the prayer
That I may follow "Jesus
   Only," everywhere.

I'm such a great big sinner,
   And still a bigger fool;
I must keep close to Jesus
And never leave His school.

My heart's so full of rapture,
   I know not how to live;
For the joy of being Jesu's
   I wish I'd more to give.

I think I'll copy Levi,
Who gave a dinner once,
To give a chance to Jesus
To save another dunce.

Oh, won't it be just "ripping"
To never leave His side,
To walk and talk with Jesus,
And all in Him confide?

There is no Friend like Jesus,
So loving, strong and true,
If I had not His friendship
I don't know what I'd do.

No soul in all creation
Can ever take His place,
But I love all others better,
Since I have seen His face.

Oh! the joy of knowing Jesus,
It takes all care away;
I would so love for Jesus
To fling my life away.

And yet I'd sooner serve Him
On earth, and suffer loss,
Than have a throne in Heaven,
For there, there's not a cross.

I love to fight for Jesus
And every risk to run,
If there was naught of danger
It wouldn't be half the fun.

Such as neglect Christ's ord'nance
To fight in lands afar,

Know not the joy of Jesus
Like those who go to war.

I loved Christ's ordination,
Its grand simplicity;
He asked no abstruse questions,
But only "Lov'st thou Me?"

He asked that once of Peter,
Who'd just denied Him thrice;
Then gave him his commission
To preach His sacrifice.

The Gospel of Christ's salvation
Is, only His blood can atone;
The secret of walking on water
Is to look to Christ alone.

The secret of power is simple,
I must obey God, not man;
It's naught but incredible folly
To adopt any other plan.

Christ commissioned His Spirit
To be Captain of His host;
I need no other guidance
Than that of the Holy Ghost.

He'll brook no interference;
God is a jealous God;
Christ woo'd and won, and bought me,
He only is my Lord.

I'll walk in His blest freedom,
And follow Him everywhere;
I'll trust His word and presence
And fight without a fear.

Some Christians call me foolish,
The world declares I'm "fey;"
I'll wait a little longer
To see what Christ will say.

"He hadn't any talents,
His speech perhaps was odd;
But he did what I commanded,
He rendered all to God."

I'd like to hear Him say that,
Tho' there's little chance of such;
But I don't care a blow
for the mud folks throw,
'Cause I'm not like a parson in church.

Some stay at home with good reason
And some without a cause;
But that coward's the worst,
who stabs in the back
The man who's gone to the wars.

But Christ was kissed in the garden
By the man who had been His friend;
So some I presume will do the same
Till this world's come to an end.

There are some who when told to go
By the great Physician Himself,
Run off to a fallible medical man
Who puts them on the shelf.

As tho' they know better than He!
Or their words were of greater worth!
They forget that the place where Jesus is
Is the safest spot on earth.

Some want to live too long,
Tho' one cannot die too soon;
A day with the Son is worth millions more
Than a million on earth or moon.

For Jesus is my life,
And death my greatest gain;
Heaven means joy without alloy,
On earth we must have pain.

If we really did believe
The words that Jesus said,
We'd have no fear for the future,
Nor for our daily bread.

Who knows Christ as his Master
Is such a splendid fool;
He leaves an earthly Paradise
And "runs away" to school!

I know very little myself,
But Jesus knows everything;
So merry of soul I laugh and sing
Underneath His wing.

Oh! it's good to belong to Jesus,
It's the only life to live;
It's glorious fun, it's heaven begun,
When you've got no more to give.

Away with hesitation!
Man! take the plunge, and try!
Give heart and all to Jesus!
Then take your wings and fly!

Fly with Christ's salvation
To some dark heathen land;
No cause for trepidation,
Jesus will hold your hand.

JESUS IS OUR MESSAGE!
JESUS SAVIOUR AND KING!
JESUS OUR SOLE COMMANDER!
JESUS IS EVERYTHING!

Come forth, ye men of Britain,
In brave Crusader bands;
Up! let us take possession
Of our Saviour's promised lands.

CHUTNEY

I want to be like Jesus,
Who left His throne on high
For hell-deserving sinners
To live, and work, and die.

Forsaking all His glory,
His power He laid aside,
His entrée — lo! a manger!
His exit — crucified!

We human fools rejected,
And left to stand alone,
The only real Victor
This world has ever known.

By men despised, rejected;
By devils deified;
By friends denied, forsaken;
By angels glorified.

I'll live and die for Jesus,
Battling for the right,
Proclaiming Christ's salvation
To sinners left and right.

I will not be a mannikin!
To live in ease at home,
I'll be a Christian warrior!
Who loves with Christ to roam.

I will not be a skulker!
Those words ring in my ear,
"Shall your brethren go to war?
And ye? shall ye sit here?"

I'd sooner be a sceptic,
Who'd ne'er confessed Christ's Name,
Than make a great confession,
But fear to play the game.

If I to others preached and taught
That consecration's right,
I wouldn't stop in Britain,
To merely talk and write.

I wouldn't say to others "Go,
The wolf needs your attentions;
Myself I'll tickle the pretty lambs
Who frequent our Conventions."

I wouldn't like to criticise
The fighters in the ring,
Unless I had the pluck to cut
Dame Europe's apron string.

I wouldn't be a talker,
With his pretty nouns and verbs,

His nicely polished phrases,
And alliterated words.

Such things may please old women,
And the maids of either sex;
They nauseate a soldier,
They irritate and vex.

For the soldier's heart is simple,
And true, and brave, and strong;
Not quite the man to tickle
With a sentimental song.

The offerings of a soldier
Are wrought of golden deeds,
He cultivates no flowers,
He reckons words as weeds.

His words are few and simple,
And giv'n with such a snap
As makes you think of lightning,
And its after thunder-clap.

For his commands are rugged,
And terse, and loud, and hoarse,
But they set the men in motion,
Artillery, foot and horse.

For his men are dead sure certain
That when they're sent to the front
Their Chief won't stay in Britain,
Shunning the battle's brunt.

For their Captain's "Go" means "Come,"
And he fights at the head of his men,
And not all the pleasures or wealth of the world,
Could tempt him to leave them then.

Thus Jesus leads the way,
As well as brings up the rear,
And He's always there in the thick of the fight,
To save, and help, and cheer.

I'm going to stake my all for Christ
Like brave Epaphroditus,
Who gambled with his life for Paul,
The prince of Christian fighters.

For how can man live better
Than gambling for the Christ,
Who lived and died for sinners,
And heaven sacrificed?

So I'll live and die for Jesus,
Battling for the right;
Proclaiming Christ's salvation
To sinners day and night.

CHRISTIAN'S DELIGHT

Now Christ's command is simple,
And meant to be obeyed,
"Go ye and preach My Gospel
In every land," He said.

Christ hadn't any favourites;
He lived and died for all!
So all should know the Message,
And hear His gracious call.

So I'll go and face the music
In some dark far off land,
Where no one's ever been before
For Christ to make a stand.

I'll leave the ninety-nine behind,
And seek the wandering sheep,
To bring it back to Jesus Christ,
And lay it at His feet.

The way may not be easy,
The grub not over good,

The climate may be treacherous,
The men a devil's brood.

But what of that? My Jesus
Suffered torture and the cross
For me the chief of sinners,
Lest I should suffer loss.

It may mean death or poverty,
Or grief-or pain-or shame,
But what of that? The martyrs lived
And suffered just the same.

I wouldn't want to live at all
Unless it was to fight
For Jesus Christ and sinful men,
Morning, noon and night.

And in some fierce, hot battle,
Fighting I'd love to die,
Watching for Jesus' coming,
To carry me home on high.

But when I walk the golden street.
I'll blush a scarlet red,
And hide my face in shame until
The crown drops off my head.

The crown that Jesus won and gave
To His unworthy son,
Who'd done so little, and badly, too,
Even the things he'd done.

And if it won't drop off I'll cast
My crown at Jesus' feet,
Then run and seek the lowest place
Upon the lowest seat.

And then I think I'll weep and weep
Till Jesus dries my eyes,
As I realise at last the depth
Of His great sacrifice.

And that I can't go back to earth,
And have another try
To serve Him better than before,
To suffer and to die.

And then I'll shout with rapture
With all the heavenly host,
"Glory to God, the Father,
The Son and Holy Ghost."

And then the joys of meeting
The loved ones gone before,
And watching for the others
To enter at the door!

My word! what introductions
To all God's family,
And leave to ask them questions
With impunity.

I'll want to hear from Jonah
Of his time inside the fish,

And how John Baptist laughed to see
His head upon the dish.

How Daniel felt descending
Into the lion's den;
What Gideon thought when marching out
With but three hundred men.

What Nebby thought about the three
Who nearly caught a cold,
When thrown into the fire because
They wouldn't worship gold.

And what they felt like when they found
That they had merely come
To have a walk with Jesus,
Who Had just arrived from Home.

We understand that Nebby got
Converted on the spot,
And right away for infidels
Began to make it hot.

We need a few like Shadrach, Meshach,
And Abednego
To pay a little visit now
To Christendom, I trow.

They'd say we were behind the times,
And just as much demented,
As poor old Uncle Nebby was
Before he had repented.

The image then was on the plain,
But now it's come to town,
And has as many votaries
To worship and bow down.

Elijah's thoughts on Carmel
When he faced the mighty throng-
My! how he chaffed the Baalites,
Laughing loud and long.

And what the Apostles felt and thought,
And what the women said,
When first they gazed on Jesus Christ
Risen, from the dead.

The comical grimaces of
Philippi's magistrates,
When they had to beg Paul's pardon
And escort him to the gates.

The thoughts of Simon Peter
When he felt the chains drop off;
And the gates began to open
Like a lion going to cough.

And why poor Rhoda's mistress thought
She'd gone stark, staring mad,
Because she said that Peter stood
Outside the door. Too bad!

The faces of the Sadducees,
When the fishermen declared

In future they'd obey the Lord,
Not men! They must have stared.

For well they knew that Peter
Had so late denied the Lord,
In mortal fear of women, too,
Though neither had a sword.

It must have been as though they saw
A Baa-lamb on its legs;
Deploring their pernicious taste
For eating addled eggs.

Their nonplussed looks, when Peter told
The godless Roman soldiers,
"Kindly crucify me, with
My head below my shoulders."

And when the oil began to boil,
The aspect of the crowd,
As John within began to sing,
And thank the Lord aloud.

In heaven no amusement?
I venture to declare
There's never been such fun on earth
As we shall have up there.

The joy will be without alloy
Within our home above,
A perfect Father's family
And every soul in love.

Enthusiastic service for
A perfect Master too,
And every servant singing,
"I want more work to do."

All hearts will glow with rapture,
As we gaze on Jesus' face,
While we sing the wondrous story,
Of the Father's matchless grace.

WITHOUT
EXCUSE

Our Saviour has given commandment
To such as believe, in their hearts,
To publish the news of Salvation
On earth, to its uttermost parts.

The doors of the world lie wide open;
Its lands have been duly explored;
The sorrows and needs of the heathen
Can only be met by the Lord.

Christians were never so numerous,
Never so wealthy and wise,
Never made bigger professions,
Then why don't we race for the prize?

Have we waxed fat like Jeshurun?
Are our livers or heads over large?
Have we become paralytic?
Or deaf to Christ's summons to charge?

When has the job been so easy?
Peace is enthroned on the earth;

Travel was never so simple;
Of "Dreadnoughts" alone there's a dearth.

How shall we look when our Saviour
Returns in His glory from heaven,
And finds we've refused or neglected
E'en one tribe with salvation to leaven?

If George the Fifth's soldiers or sailors
Were ordered the world to subdue,
They'd hasten abroad in dead earnest
And pluckily dare and do.

Then why should the Soldiers of Jesus
Delay to obey His command?
Come along! Let us tackle the business,
We only need faith and sand.
("sand" means "courage")

Come! Let's stop our vain talk of traditions,
Which nullify God's Holy Word,
And dump all our Christless snobbery
In hell, and then hurry abroad.

Let us cease to do our own pleasure,
Stop hoarding and living at ease;
Let us fight or die to deliver
The folk in the lands overseas.

Let's abolish our tame stonewalling,
And play for a win not a draw;
We must go in for hurricane hitting,
Or we'll lose as we've lost before.

For Christ was a resolute hitter,
And so were Stephen and Paul;
They so warmed the devil's fingers
That he scarce could hold the ball.

They didn't play selfish in those good days,
They played for their side instead;
And they ran such really impossible runs
That the devil quite lost his head.

When a man got out he ran, not walked,
And the man going in ran too;
"What, stop the match for tea!" they cried;
"Bah! cock-a-doodle-doo."

They didn't wear pads or gloves those days,
You just couldn't make them afraid;
And they never stopped to look at the clock
Till the winning hit was made.

Now if we played the game like that,
Do you think we shouldn't win?
Of course we should, and, that being so,
Anything else is sin.

Christ to be sure would go with us;
Christ would see us through;
Christ wouldn't let us falter
Till there's nothing more to do.

So let's settle now and once for all,
To finish our job or die;
We can evangelize the world
If we're men enough to try.

GOD'S DD

Old Daniel was a Dreadnought!
If he was here to-day,
He'd make it hot for the pious lot
Who don't do as they say.

He didn't speak behind folks' backs,
But met them face to face;
He called spades spades, and dubbed knaves knaves,
And always proved his case.

He neither cared for place nor power,
Nor feared the lions' den;
A godly cause will lock the jaws
Of beasts, or jealous men.

Whatever God at any time
Might write upon the wall,
He'd up and say, without delay,
To King and Court and all.

Dan didn't say "Belshazzar, Sire,
Your faults are peccadilloes";
He hit his sin with a rolling pin,
And not with feather pillows.

Dan didn't sugar-coat his pills,
Half doses didn't please him;
To save a life he'd use the knife
And bleed a fool to ease him.

Old Daniel ran a college once
Which turned out three invincibles;
A verse or two will let you know
What things he taught as principles.

Dare to be a Dreadnought,
With purpose true and firm;
Dare to live on simple fare,
And don't become a worm.

Dare to be a Dreadnought,
Dare to beard a King;
Tell him all the truth and don't
Emasculate the thing.

Dare to be a Dreadnought,
Faithful, loyal, bold,
Scorning under any threats
To worship man or gold.

Dare to be a Dreadnought,
Not a dressed up "toff,"
Nor glorified policeman,
Nor gun that won't go off.

Make a bold confession,
Though it means the rod;
Dare to kick the devil hard,
And dare to trust in God.

C.T. STUDD
QUOTES

Some wish to live within the sound of church or chapel bell. I want to run a rescue shop within a yard of hell.

• • • • •

Let us not glide through this world and then slip quietly into heaven, without having blown the trumpet loud and long for our Redeemer, Jesus Christ. Let us see to it that the devil will hold a thanksgiving service in hell, when he gets the news of our departure from the field of battle.

• • • • •

We will not build on the sand, but on the bedrock of the sayings of Christ, and the gates and minions of hell shall not prevail against us. Should such men as we fear? Before the world, aye, before the sleepy, lukewarm, faithless, namby-pamby Christian world, we will dare to trust our God, we will venture our all for Him, we will live and we will die for Him, and we will do it with His joy unspeakable singing aloud in our hearts. We will a thousand times sooner die trusting only our God, than live trusting in man. And when we come to this position the battle is already won, and the end of the glorious campaign in sight. We will have the real Holiness of God, not the sickly stuff of talk and dainty words and pretty thoughts; we will have a Masculine Holiness, one of daring faith and works for Jesus Christ.

• • • • •

How could I spend the best years of my life in living for the honours of this world, when thousands of souls are perishing every day?

• • • • •

Difficulties, dangers, disease, death, or divisions don't deter any but Chocolate Soldiers from executing God's Will. When someone says there is a lion in the way, the real Christian promptly replies, "That's hardly enough inducement for me; I want a bear or two besides to make it worth my while to go."

• • • • •

Funds are low again, hallelujah! That means God trusts us and is willing to leave His reputation in our hands.

• • • • •

The best cure for discouragement or qualms is another daring plunge of faith.

• • • • •

How little chance the Holy Ghost has nowadays. The churches and missionary societies have so bound Him in red tape that they practically ask Him to sit in a corner while they do the work themselves.

• • • • •

The time is so short, such a little time to rescue souls from hell, for there will be no rescue work in heaven.

• • • • •

If Jesus Christ be God and died for me, then no sacrifice can be too great for me to make for Him.

• • • • •

The best training for a soldier of Christ is not merely a theological college. They always seem to turn out sausages of varying lengths, tied at each end, without the glorious freedom a Christian ought to abound and rejoice in. You see, when in hand-to-hand conflict with the world and the devil, neat little biblical confectionery is like shooting lions with a pea-shooter: one needs a man who will let himself go and deliver blows right and left as hard as he can hit, trusting in the Holy Ghost. It's experience, not preaching that hurts the devil and confounds the world. The training is not that of the schools but of the market: it's the hot, free heart and not the balanced head that knocks the devil out. Nothing but forked-lightning Christians will count. A lost reputation is the best degree for Christ's service. It is not so much the degree of arts that is needed, but that of hearts, loyal and true, that love not their lives to the death: large and loving hearts which seek to save the lost multitudes, rather than guard the ninety-nine well-fed sheep in the pen.

• • • • •

I am getting desperately afraid of going to heaven for I have had the vision of the shame I shall suffer as I get my first glimpse of the Lord Jesus; His majesty, power and marvellous love for me, who treated Him so meanly and shabbily on earth, and acted as though I did Him a favour in serving Him! No wonder God shall have to wipe away the tears off all faces, for we shall be broken-hearted when we see the depth of His love and the shallowness of ours.

• • • • •

Our recruits come out from home vastly raw and are largely parrots. They have been crammed with religion as though for an examination, and seem to come out to carry on their education rather than finish it. So many are just taught doctrines without ever having thought them out or searched the Scriptures for themselves. They come out like infants with pop-guns. They need to be trained into soldiers with real devil-defying weapons. Some arrive thinking they are the last thing in high-class Christianity and have to find out they know little.

That is why I keep the newcomers here at base for a time till I can make them really think out things and settle questions, not from hearsay but from Bible-say.

•••••

Don't go into the study to prepare a sermon — that's nonsense. Go into your study to God and get so fiery that your tongue is like a burning coal and you have got to speak.

•••••

Marriage can be a great blessing or a great curse, depending on where you place the Cross.

•••••

I realized that my life was to be one of simple, childlike faith, and that my part was to trust, not to do. I was to trust in Him and He would work in me to do His good pleasure. From that time my life was different.

•••••

We Christians too often substitute prayer for playing the game. Prayer is good; but when used as a substitute for obedience, it is nothing but a blatant hypocrisy, a despicable Pharisaism... To your knees, man! and to your Bible! Decide at once! Don't hedge! Time flies! Cease your insults to God, quit consulting flesh and blood. Stop your lame, lying, and cowardly excuses. Enlist!

• • • • •

Believing that further delay would be sinful, some of
God's insignificants and nobodies in particular, but
trusting in our Omnipotent God, have decided on
certain simple line, according to the Book of God, to
make a definite attempt to render the evangelization
of the world an accomplished fact. For this purpose
we have banded together under the name of "Christ's
Etceteras," and invite others of God's people to join
us in this glorious enterprise. We are merely Christ's
nobodies, otherwise Christ's Etceteras. We rejoice in
and thank God for the good work being carried on in
the already occupied lands by God's Regular Forces.
We seek to attack and win to Christ only those parts
the devil's empire which are beyond the extremest
outposts of the regular army of God. Christ's Etceteras
are a union mission; a Christian, and, therefore,
an international brotherhood; a supplementary
Worldwide Evangelization Crusade.

• • • • •

Too long have we been waiting for one another to
begin! The time of waiting is past! The hour of God
has struck! War is declared! In God's Holy Name let us
arise and build! 'The God of Heaven, He will fight for
us', as we for Him. We will not build on the sand, but
on the bedrock of the sayings of Christ, and the gates
and minions of hell shall not prevail against us. Should
such men as we fear?

Get more encouragement for the battle at deeperChristian.com

Made in the USA
Coppell, TX
08 September 2022

82822299R00046